Camera Guide

----- ✥✥✥ -----

Learn What Your Digital Camera Has to Offer

George Stone

© Copyright 2017 by George Stone
- All rights reserved.

The following eBook is reproduced below with the goal of providing information that is as accurate and as reliable as possible. Regardless, purchasing this eBook can be seen as consent to the fact that both the publisher and the author of this book are in no way experts on the topics discussed within, and that any recommendations or suggestions made herein are for entertainment purposes only. Professionals should be consulted as needed before undertaking any of the action endorsed herein.

This declaration is deemed fair and valid by both the American Bar Association and the Committee of Publishers Association and is legally binding throughout the United States.

Furthermore, the transmission, duplication or reproduction of any of the following work, including precise information, will be considered an illegal act, irrespective whether it is done electronically or in print. The legality extends to creating a secondary or tertiary copy of the work or a recorded copy and is only allowed with an express written consent of the Publisher. All additional rights are reserved.

The information in the following pages is broadly considered to be a truthful and accurate account of facts, and as such any inattention, use or misuse of the information in question by the reader will render any resulting actions solely under their purview. There are no scenarios in which the publisher or the original author of this work can be in any fashion deemed liable for any hardship or damages that may befall them after undertaking information described herein.

Additionally, the information found on the following pages is intended for informational purposes only and should thus be considered, universal. As befitting its nature, the information presented is without assurance regarding its continued validity or interim quality. Trademarks that mentioned are done without written consent and can in no way be considered an endorsement from the trademark holder.

Contents

Introduction 1

Chapter 1: Types of Digital Cameras 5

Chapter 2: How to Choose Your Digital Camera 11

Chapter 3: Learning How to Use Your First DSLR 23

Chapter 4: Basics of Photography 35

Chapter 5: Composition Guidelines 41

Chapter 6: Useful Photo Editing Software 51

Conclusion 61

Introduction

Quality digital cameras are now affordable compared to when it first came out a few years ago when only professional photographers could afford one and make use of its full features. But because of their affordability, many amateurs and avid hobbyists find themselves with the DSLR hoping to pursue their hobby and interest.

There are many different types of digital cameras and purchasing one depends entirely on what you want to do with it unless of course, money is not an issue. To many people, smartphone cameras do the job of taking photos of practically everything and anything but what if you want to take your pictures to another level. Is the iPhone 7 enough?

In this book, we will look into the various types of digital cameras, what is composition, composition techniques as well as the features of digital cameras. But first, a little history?

A short history of Digital Cameras

The earliest version of a consumer centered digital camera that was compatible with a desktop PC using a USB cable was the Apple QuickTake 100 camera launched on 17 February 1994, followed by the Kodak DC40 camera launched on 28 March 1995, and then the Casio QV-11 that came with an LCD monitor in late 1995.

Camera Guide

Of all, the Sony Cyber-Shot Digital Still Camera that came in 1996 became the most famous at that time. When Kodak came in aggressively to the digital camera market, they pushed the idea of digital photography to the mass market.

Microsoft worked with Kodak to create kiosks that enabled consumers to print or edit digital images and create their own Photo CD discs. These kiosks could also add digital images to any documents.

IBM followed up with Kodak collaboration in building a network image transfer via the Internet. Hewlett-Packard became the first company to produce printers with color inkjet technology which complimented the new digital camera images.

This technology and the applications surrounding it has changed the way we use digital cameras.

The great thing about DSLRs is that it is pretty easy to use. Most of the time, for people looking to take good pictures but do not want to go through the hassle of learning the entirety of a DSLR.

So, using the AUTO function and immediately starting to photograph would render beautiful images- that is the beauty of the DSLR compared to the older non-digital models.

However, you are probably wondering what all those little icons on the camera are for and what they do. This book will give you the most fundamental details of using the digital camera technology that you now own and take your photos from 'nice' to 'amazing' in a few simple clicks, positioning, and using the right settings.

Introduction

This book will cover things like lens filters and Aperture, Shutter speed, ISO as well as Composition that will help you make the most of your camera and produce beautiful and stunning images.

But before we move on, one of the most important things to do is to read your camera manual. It is something boring and something nobody wants to do (who reads manuals anyway, pfft!) but it can prove to be a valuable source of information. While most cameras come with more or less the same features, some newer cameras come with enhanced features which would be available only if you read the manual and understand what these new features are and how to use them.

Not only will the manual give you an understanding of the piece of equipment you've purchased, but it will also tell you where the buttons are located and how to get to your menus - these kinds of things are specific to camera models which this book will not cover.

While you do not need to read the whole manual, just browsing through it and getting a general sense of the information that is in it is ideal for starters. You can then read in detail the parts or sections which may help you such as camera settings, battery issues, the location of buttons, basic settings, and shooting modes, how to use them and how to change them, and when you use your camera.

Keep your manual in the bag that the camera comes in at all times so you can refer to it at any point. Sometimes, you could be flipping through the manual to find info on something else only to find something new that you never knew your camera could do. Photography is a learning process that never ends anyway.

Camera Guide

The goal of reading this book as well as your manual is to learn how to use your camera without the Auto function. It is like baking a cake from scratch instead of using a cake mix from a box- you can taste the difference, and in the camera's case, you can see (and possibly feel) the difference.

The Auto function is great only when you already have good lighting and bright scenes, and you want to capture something quick, but in low light or nighttime, the Auto function fails to produce the desired effect.

Think of the Auto function as an emergency button when you can click to take a quick shot of something that is happening right at that moment. Sometimes it is always good to have a shot of something rather than nothing at all. That said, once you go through the different functions and settings of your camera, changing these functions quickly to suit the needs would become second-nature, and you'd find yourself clicking, switching, and flicking things so fast you'd forget the Auto function was even there.

Most cameras also come with semi-auto modes such as the Aperture priority, Portrait or Landscape mode, Shutter priority and so on. We will discuss this more in detail in the book. So, read up what you can in your camera's manual before proceeding with the next chapter.

Chapter 1:

Types of Digital Cameras

It may be a daunting task to buy a digital camera, let alone choose one that fits your needs and your budget. Mostly all types of commercial cameras in market existence right now can be categorized into four main categories:

- Digital SLR (popularly referred to as DSLR)

- Point-and-Shoot

- Bridge cameras

- Camera phones

Each of these types has its advantages and disadvantages and it entirely depends on your needs. It is safe to say that right now, everyone owns a smartphone with excellent camera capabilities but what if you want better features? Take a look at the list below to understand the various types of digital cameras and their pros and cons.

1. Camera phone

Many smartphones have amazing built-in cameras, built-in that make photo taking easy. With many image-heavy apps already in the market, smartphones are always evolving to

Camera Guide

make it easier for consumers to take beautiful pictures and upload them on Facebook, Twitter, Instagram, Tumblr, and so on. Besides, the convenience of a camera phone is unbeatable.

PROS	**CONS**
• Extremely portable	• Does not have many features as high-end cameras
• You can carry it with you anywhere so you can capture unexpected moments.	• Depending on the phone you use, the quality of images may vary
• Sharing photos to social media is easy with camera phones easy to share photos right after taking them	• Most camera phones don't produce good photos in low light

Chapter 1- Types of Digital Cameras

2. Point-And-Shoot Cameras

Point-And-Shoot cameras are your average compact cameras that are designed to be convenient to carry with you in your bag, they are also affordable and they are lightweight and easy to use.

PROS	CONS
• More affordable than DSLRs	• May not be better than a good camera phone and not as high quality as DSLRs
• Have special features such as smile detection and red-eye removal	• Not as portable as a camera phone
• Newer models come with Wi-Fi connection ability so you can easily share photos	• No interchangeable lenses

3. Bridge Cameras

Bridge cameras come somewhere between their point-and-shoot cousins and the DSLRs. Bridge cameras are also sometimes called super-zooms.

PROS	CONS
• Much higher quality than point-and-shoot cameras	• Not as compact. Bulkier than point-and-shoot versions
• Has plenty of the same functions as a DSLR	• Has a smaller sensor compared to DSLR. Not very good quality.
• Comes with magnificent zoom lens functions	• Also, does not come with interchangeable lenses

4. Interchangeable Mirrorless Lens Camera

Want a pocket sized DSLR alternative? Then you can get the mirrorless lens camera that comes with interchangeable lenses.

PROS	CONS
• Takes good quality images and often a preferred version to bulky DSLRs	• Expensive than point-and-shoot cameras
• Lightweight and portable	• Zoom lens that comes with the camera is lesser than bridge cameras
• Can switch lenses and settings to give you advanced creative control	• Buying more lenses will incur costs and won't make your camera portable

Camera Guide

5. DSLR

Abbreviation for Digital Single-Lens Reflex, this is a large camera that comes with interchangeable lenses and usually preferred to take high-end and high-quality photos.

PROS	CONS
• Gives you excellent images of high-quality	• The most expensive compared to all other digital cameras
• Greater quality control with advanced settings and ability to change lenses	• Definitely not portable and requires different lenses
• Has large sensors that enable you to take good quality photos in low-light scenarios	• More difficult to learn for beginners

Chapter 2:

How to Choose Your Digital Camera

Cameras have evolved tremendously with technology, and it makes purchasing a camera simple and easy too. Plus, it has become a lot more affordable. However, centuries later, we are lucky to have plenty of choices to choose from. Like buying a house or a car or even a bag, getting the right camera to fit your needs requires some thoughtful planning too.

So many essential elements come into the decision-making process from price, quality of the image, purpose of taking photographs, and so on. In this chapter, we will look into how best to purchase a new camera and hopefully the tips and details in this section will help point you make the right purchasing decision for your needs and budget.

1. Point-And-Shoot Cameras

As mentioned in the previous chapter, point-and-shoot cameras are compact cameras that are straightforward, easy to use, and affordable. If you plan on getting something like this, they are in the range of $100 to $200, and while their image quality is not stellar, they do offer more creative control than smartphone cameras.

Camera Guide

Look for cameras that come with zoom lenses, Wi-Fi connectivity as well as image stabilization. Some point-and-shoot cameras also come as standard megazooms and compact megazooms and these versions start at $200 to $500. Megazoom versions give you plenty of shooting flexibility.

2. Bridge Cameras

The bigger and more expensive megazooms are also known as Bridge cameras, and they come with longer lenses and an almost full-featured, with DSLR type bodies. However, they still have shooting quality and performance of a compact camera, because of their small sensors. If you want better quality, then choose an advanced compact bridge camera with at least a 1" type sensor.

This can cost you as little as $500 to as much as $1500. Bigger sensors bring in more light producing better photos. The only downside to this is that it makes your bridge cameras building

3. Interchangeable mirrorless lens camera

You'd want to get this if superior image quality is what you are looking for, plus with added creative options. However, they come with a hefty price. Mirrorless cameras are an attractive alternative to DSLRs.

Mirrorless because they do not have the bulky mirror and the optical viewfinder that you see in DSLRs. Prices of mirror-less cameras begin at $500, and it can go up to a few thousand. The larger the sensor, the more expensive it will be.

4. DSLR

You would often find that DSLR cameras come in the same price range that you find your mirror-less cameras in. Top of

Chapter 2- How to Choose Your Digital Camera

the line models starts at a cool $6,500. The quality of an image is the same as a mirrorless but what sets a DSLR apart is the added benefits that come with it.

Professional photographers still prefer DSLRs and for a good reason. They come with the principal features such as autofocus which are better at tracking moving objects, a superior optical viewfinder that provides a clear view of any subject in any lighting condition and DSLRs also have better battery life. DSLRs can push at least 1,000 shots, and finally, DSLRs also have better build quality. They have solid construction making them have weather sealing, and they also have the ultimate ruggedness and durability.

Understanding the basics features of each camera can already give you an idea of what kind of camera you want and how it fits your needs.

How much do you want to pay?

Ideally, you want to spend based on how much you use your camera. Is it for leisure purposes? Going on a holiday and you want really good pictures? Or are you looking to invest more in your photography hobby? Are you planning on becoming a part-time or freelance photographer? Do you just want a camera that is easy to carry but still take good pictures?

As the saying goes - you get what you pay for. So, the biggest consideration on how much to spend entirely depends on how often you will use the camera and what your needs are.

Some expensive models are loaded with extra features, but these features may be something you may never use. Also, most people are practically happy with smartphone cameras such as ones from iPhones and Samsung that offer superior quality photos in good lighting.

What about shutter speed?

Shutter speed is important but most cameras these days are adequately fast. Those that offer better performance as cameras with an interchangeable lens such as the mirrorless and DSLRs because they will make focusing faster and tracking subjects easier and takes more photos per second, typically more than ten frames per second (fps).

The average point-and-shoot versions cannot capture more than two or three frames per second.

What about ergonomics?

Trying your camera before you buy is important. You want to make sure the camera is comfortable to hold and isn't so heavy it puts you off from carrying it around. This will happen, and sooner or later you'd find yourself happy with just your smartphone camera.

Whatever camera you choose to get whether the simple point-and-shoot or the bulky advanced DSLR, you want to offer quick accessibility for standard and most used features and functions. Your camera shouldn't be too complicated to get it up and operating, and menus should be at a logical and structured position on your camera so you can quickly switch settings or turn on functions.

Newer models also come touchscreen functions increasing the accessibility option. However, it can be frustrating if controls and menus are all over the place, making it harder for you to calibrate.

Chapter 2- How to Choose Your Digital Camera

Of course, all of this depends on you. You must find it easy to touch, hold and navigate your camera.

Does having high megapixels help?

We all hear how marketers advertise the megapixels in a camera which makes you think that that is the most important feature for high-quality images. Reading your camera specifications is ideal, and when you do, you will notice that DSLRs as well as point-and-shoot offer the same megapixel count which is about 16MP or 20MP and so on.

However, make no mistake and say that they are the same. Overall performance and quality vary significantly between the two cameras. Compact cameras are equipped with smaller imaging sensors, and while they do an excellent job in taking pictures, they create a lot of noise in low light.

When you use interchangeable lens cameras, you will encounter less noise because they have much larger sensors and work perfectly in low-light situations, giving you a better-quality photo all together. You can shoot in dim-lighting without flash, and there will be less image degradation.

Also, if you are shooting to print large images, then you would need interchangeable lenses. The bottom line, when purchasing a camera; do not look at the megapixel count alone because there are other factors that provide different results. The quality of image sensor, optics, and physical size play a much more important role in producing good images.

Megapixel counts especially if you want to crop large pictures or print them, but it has no connection with the quality of the image itself.

Camera Guide

Do I need the interchangeable lens?

There are a few things that set apart a good camera from a great one, and that would be the lens. A camera without its lens is useless, and that is why the interchangeable lens is a much sought-after feature in many avid photographers and professionals. Think of interchangeable lens as tailor-made suits- you can tailor make your camera to meet your creative needs and give you loads of shooting options. The interchangeable lens offers so much more versatility.

The interchangeable lens can be found in primary 18 to 55mm lens, and they are often called a kit lens. From there on, you can add-on your lens as how a makeup artist adds brushes. You can find the wide-angle lens, macro lens as well as super telephoto lens to name a few. However, not all lenses are interchangeable with any camera. Canon lenses are designed for Canon cameras, Kodak lenses for Kodak cameras and Nikon lenses for Nikon cameras. Only some lenses can be used on a variety of different camera models. However, you are better off purchasing a lens that is designed specifically for your camera model.

What about digital and optical zoom?

Just like megapixels, optical zooms are a feature you shouldn't be too worried about when buying or choosing a camera. Camera brands like throw photography jargon around to entice buyers thinking that optical zooms make images crisper and clearer. The truth is, the camera captures no more extra detail whether using digital zoom or optical zoom. Optical zoom utilizes real optics, so you are closer to your subject and whereas the digital zoom employs the same method except it crops and image and blows it up to fill the original photo size.

Chapter 2- How to Choose Your Digital Camera

So next time a marketer goes on about optical zoom, pay less attention to it.

What should I know about display screens?

Manufacturers of cameras nowadays pay close attention to display screen sizes because it makes it easier to visualize a subject. While this is important, other factors must be taken into consideration too. For example, the resolution size of a display determines how clear the screen looks. Most cameras come with a large screen display anyway which usually ranges between three to five inches, and the resolution is sufficient. However, as technology becomes better other forms of display options become available, such as OLED which makes displays look even better and brighter. Before deciding on the type of screen, whether it is LCD or OLED, check the resolution of the screen first.

Another factor to look into would be touchscreens. Not all cameras require them, and you would find that most camera brands do not come with touch screens either. Like mirrorless cameras, touchscreen displays are excellent for selecting a focus point and also triggering your shutter. Touchscreen simplifies the process of navigating between menus and, since people are already tuned in to using touchscreens on smartphones, it just makes the finger action a lot easier on cameras through swiping between menus and functions.

Do I need a viewfinder in my camera?

Having a viewfinder definitely, brings in a set of benefits to the photographer and if you ask around, many photographers still find that the viewfinder is better than an LCD screen. Mirrorless cameras use EVF- electronic viewfinders whereas DSLRs use the optical viewfinder. Point-and-shoot cameras generally do not have EVFs because they add to the camera's weight as well as size. The viewfinder is a matter of personal preference so if you are new to photography; you may find that the touchscreen suits you better since you are probably used to swiping.

What about video options?

All brands of cameras record videos these days from point-and-shoot to DSLRs and some even record 4K in Ultra HD resolution. The DSLRs and Mirrorless versions can even be used for filmmaking and is a favorite for YouTube videos and amateur filmmaking.

The most important thing for video shooting using a camera would be stabilization. A camera with IBIS or lens that comes with OIS is your best option if you do not want the hassle of carrying around a tripod. IBIS and OIS functions ensure that your video is smooth, less noise and you obtain non-jittery footage when you take videos by hand.

What other specifications should I look out for?

a) Shooting modes

If you want good, high-quality images than advanced compacts and interchangeable cameras are what you need to look for. If you don't want to mess around with apertures, shutter speed and ISO then stick with the point-and-shoot versions. While DSLRs and Mirrorless also offer you auto modes, you can still have full creative control on your cameras and only switch to auto if you need to take pictures in a split second.

Chapter 2- How to Choose Your Digital Camera

b) RAW vs. JPEG

Most cameras will shoot in JPEG mode, and that is great because computer formats and smartphones and social media usually go by JPEG too. However, cameras on the high-end with the interchangeable lens can also produce images in RAW. RAW images retain the full details from your camera's sensor, and it does not throw any data away as JPEGs do. The quality of the picture doesn't change whether it is JPEG or RAW but with RAW images, it helps with post production. With a RAW image, editing is a much easier process as things can be changed. For example, saturations can be adjusted, color balanced changed, highlights can be lowered down, and shadows can be brightened.

This extra information from a photo is expensive because RAW files are much bigger files than high-quality JPEG - almost four times larger. This means you need to have a large-capacity memory card to hold all the images you are taking as well as enough hard drive space for you to store your pictures. Your computer also needs to have higher memory and RAM to be able to edit the images.

c) Wi-Fi & GPS

Mostly, all cameras nowadays have a Wi-Fi feature because the need to share images quickly has become a necessity especially with the prevalence of social media. Modern cameras have the ability to easily share photographed images from the camera to social media without the need of plugging in your camera to a PC or laptop. GPS isn't considered a necessity, unlike Wi-Fi. But to those who love taking quality photos of the places they visit, then geotagging is probably a feature you want. GPS is usually an optional add-on if you want it in your camera but keep in mind that with GPS running in the background of your

Camera Guide

camera, your battery is going to drain faster so it might not be a good option for traveling either unless you're okay with plugging around a charger.

d)   Waterproofing and weatherproofing

If the manufacturer claims that the camera is weatherproof, rainproof, splash proof, and shockproof - it is NOT waterproof. These simply mean that the buttons and seams of your camera have been sealed off to keep water and mist from getting in. But as we all know in the age of smartphones, if your camera falls into the water and gets submerged- then you need to get your rice out. If you use your camera for capturing outdoor events, news coverage, and activities in different terrains then you need to make sure that your camera is waterproof. Waterproof cameras are designed for underwater use, literally, to be submerged so you can take photos while you snorkel!

Most DSLRs are weatherproof and also shockproof. They can be utilized for outdoor photography even if there are light rain and snow or moisture present and it won't be damaged. Mist from waterfalls or even splashing from small waves will not damage the camera. However, if you have any doubts ask people who use the brand that you have, and the best place to go would be to forums.

Also take note that while your camera may be weatherproof, your lens may not be. However, you may be able to purchase waterproof cases for your lenses, and these are often pretty expensive. Most cameras nowadays are also designed to be shockproof so they can survive a small drop.

Conclusion

Your budget will also determine the camera that you ultimately choose. However, both needs and budget go hand in hand so picking a camera as a standalone if you do not have much budget may be the best way to go especially for amateurs and novice photographers. You do not need to buy a high-end camera at the get-go. The goal is to understand the basics of a camera before purchasing any other additional features. Ultimately, a DSLR or mirrorless camera would be a good option if quality and fast response are what you seek, plus if you have the monies to spend.

Chapter 3:

Learning How to Use Your First DSLR

The DSLR may seem intimidating from all the other types of digital cameras out there, and this is only because of the number of buttons and icons and dials not to mention the manual that comes with it.

But as mentioned in the introduction, reading the manual is very important, however, no matter how tempting it may be to just leave it out of your DSLR education and click on Auto to begin your photography journey, learning what you can do with your DSLR puts you in charge of creative control as opposed to giving this power to your DSLR.

In this chapter, we will go through the basics that are available on almost every DSLR camera. Take note that this is not your manual replacement rather it briefly explains to you the essential functions and features that would ultimately lead you to read your manual to find out more about the particular camera that you have because there is a lot to learn if you want to get the most of your DSLR.

Camera Guide

1. Shooting Modes

Shooting modes are probably the first few things you will notice on your camera be it a DSLR or the average digital point-and-shoot camera. Shooting modes are labeled on a round mode dial with 'Auto, Av, Tv, P, and M.' Depending on your camera, there might be other modes too, and other abbreviations used instead such as A, S, P and M. But they all function the same way. That is why it is important to read your manual.

Adjusting your shooting type will regulate the way your camera would behave when you click on the shutter. Take for instance, if you clicked on the auto function the camera will have preset details on exposure, shutter speed as well as aperture- all you need to do is click.

The other modes are:

Av for Aperture Priority- also labeled as A, aperture priority or known as a 'semi-automatic' method. When this function is clicked on, the photographer sets the aperture, and the shutter speed is mechanically decided by the camera.

Aperture is the volume of the lens opening through which light passes through each time the shutter opens. The bigger the aperture, the higher the content of light that passes through it. Aperture directly relates to the influences the depth of field which how much of the image that is in focus. Aperture is a significant feature in photography and having a large depth of field means you have a large distance to focus. Using the aperture priority ensures that you can control the depth of field while other components are calculated by the camera.

Chapter 3- Learning How to Use Your First DSLR

Tv for Shutter Priority- also labeled as S, refers to another type of semi-automatic shooting mode except for this feature, the photographer sets the shutter speed, and the camera looks after the aperture function. Shutter speed is calibrated in seconds, and it is determined by the length of time the shutter is required to open when a photo is being taken.

The prolonged the shutter remains open; the more light goes through the sensors in the camera that will be obtained.

Shutter and aperture are instrumental modes to shoot that give any photographer the creative control to determine how they would like to shoot their picture and subjects the way they vision them, giving them a form of creative control despite using semi-automatic functions.

P for Program – this mode is in the middle between full manual control and the semi-automatic functions of the shutter and aperture. Using the program mode will enable you to set either the shutter speed or aperture speed, and the camera will work on maintaining the right amount of exposure by adjusting accordingly. This gives the photographer the additional creative control on whether to use shutter priority or aperture priority without the need of switching between either mode.

M for Manual- The manual mode gives you overall control over exposure, allowing you to set both aperture and shutter speed on your own. You will typically see the exposure indicator either on your screen or in the viewfinder which will tell you how over-exposed or underexposed your image will be. You can then adjust the shutter speed or the aperture yourself so that you accomplish the right amount of exposure.

Camera Guide

2. Understanding ISO

ISO refers to the sensitivity of your camera sensor to light. The ISO sensitivity is given through numerical representation where ISO 100 refers to low sensitivity, and ISO 6400 is high sensitivity. ISO determines the quantity of light required by the camera's sensor to obtain a certain degree of exposure. More light is required during low sensitivities to accomplish the right level of exposure compared to when less light is required during high sensitivity to obtain the same degree of exposure as during low light.

Here are two different situations to explain how ISO works:

- Low ISO numbers

  When the light conditions are good such as on a radiant day, there will be plenty of usable light that will hit the sensor during an exposure. This results in the sensor not needing to be highly sensitive to obtain the right balance of exposure. During these situations, a low ISO number is utilized which is between ISO 100 to ISO 200. Your images will turn out in excellent quality with very little to no noise or grain.

- High ISO numbers

  On the off chance that shooting in low light conditions, for example, inside a dull house of prayer or a dimly lit club, for instance, there is very little light accessible for your camera sensor. A high ISO number, for example, ISO 3200, will expand the sensitivity of the sensor, viably increasing the little measure of available light to give you an accurately exposed picture. This augmentation impact accompanies a symptom of

Chapter 3- Learning How to Use Your First DSLR

expanded noise on the image, which resembles a fine grain, decreasing the general picture quality. The noise will be most articulated in the darker/shadow areas.

The idea is to keep your ISO as low as you possibly can.

- The lesser the ISO, the higher the quality of the image
- On a sunny day, an ISO 200 does an excellent job
- On cloudy days, select ISO of between 400 to 800
- For shooting indoors when the light is low, select an ISO of around 1600

Plenty of DSLRs these days come equipped with an auto ISO function which makes the photographer's job slightly easier. The camera decides on the ISO setting by relying on the amount of light that comes to its sensor. The camera will endeavor to keep the ISO as low as can be.

This auto-ISO function help novice photographers considerably as it helps the photographer determine and define the furthest breaking point. This breaking point refers to the situation where the images are extremely noisy such as when it is set at ISO 1600 to ISO 3200.

The photographer has the choice of leaving it as it is until the situation comes where you need to override manually the automatic setting. This happens when the photographer takes a landscape shot utilizing a tripod stand. Low ISO settings for this situation is possible.

Camera Guide

3. Learning the 'Exposure Triangle'

The exposure triangle relates to shutter speed, ISO and of course aperture. They all control:

- The amount of light entering the camera (aperture and shutter speed)

- The amount of light needed by the camera (ISO)

Understanding these three elements and how they are linked and the relationship between them is vital to ensure you have the right creative control over your camera. Changing either of these settings will impact the other two. It is the case of balancing these books to get the best results.

4. Mastering Metering

Metering refers to the camera's assessment of an entire scene in light and dark areas and determining the exposure so that all tones within the overall image equates to an average 18% gray. This gray is called middle gray.

Similarly, if you point to shoot your camera at a dark scene, the photograph of the resulting image will be brighter than you see it. The scene is always being averaged by your camera and more often than not, the image is correctly exposed.

If you want to control what areas are being assessed by the camera, then you need to influence the method in which the exposure is metered.

There are three metering modes that you can choose from:

- Average – In this situation, the camera quantifies the whole tone of the picture frame from one corner to the

Chapter 3- Learning How to Use Your First DSLR

other and the scene is exposed to 18% gray as a result of this quantification.

- Centre-weighted – For this situation, the camera quantifies the exposure reading taken from the center of the viewfinder, which is about 80% of the entire image. The extreme corners of the image are not counted.

- Spot metering – Minimal scene is used in this situation to quantify the amount of exposure needed. This is typically a small circle in the middle of the viewfinder. The total image taken is only 5%. The camera will quantify the dark/light tones in this area and expose the entire scene to 18% gray, from that assessment.

When you first start out with your camera, a good starting point is average, or center weighted metering. These two will give you an adequate, consistent measure of exposure required for your photo, and if you choose one mode and stick to it, you will soon come to the understanding of how it looks like when a scene is underexposed or overexposed compared to when you see it in real life. So, what can you do if a scene is over or underexposed? This is where the crucial element of exposure compensation is needed.

5. **Learn to Focus**

No matter what kind of shooting mode you choose, or what amount of ISO you determine, there will be a subject in your frame that you want to focus on. When you do not fully achieve the right focus, your resulting image will not turn out the way you want it to be. There are different focusing modes that you can choose to ensure you get the right focal point:

Camera Guide

- AF-S (autofocus-single) commonly used for stationary objects such as portraits, buildings, and landscape. A half-press motion is used on the shutter which would result in acquiring the focus. The focus will lock on that point for the entire time that the button is pressed down. If you want to modify to focus, you need to let go the button, recompose and then re-half-press.

- AF-C (autofocus-continuous) commonly used for moving objects and subjects such as during sporting activities and animals. By semi-pressing the shutter, the focus will be attained and locked onto a given subject. The moment the subject moves, the focus will readjust and it will continue to refocus until the photograph has been snapped by clicking on the button.

Both these focus modes also rely on focus points. Focus points are the numbers of squares or dots that you can see in your viewfinder which is laid across the screen. The minute you half-press the shutter, you can see one of these squares flash in red. That is known as the active focus point, and that is the position that the frame will focus on.

6. Determining File Size and Types

You can also edit the size of your images that your camera records the photos in. If you want a file size that is the largest possible, then you need to ensure that you make the most of your megapixels that you have invested in.

You can choose RAW or JPEG modes.

The RAW file is bigger and uncompressed, and it contains valuable image data that allows flexibility during post-processing. The JPEG file is a compressed file that is usually

Chapter 3- Learning How to Use Your First DSLR

the standard file that the camera processes images in. These images are print ready, meaning no processing is required. These files are much smaller and can hold a lot of images on your memory card.

If you are starting out, then using JPEG is the most standard way to go. It will enable you to see the best results while you explore the basics of photography and using your camera before you complicate things with RAW files.

7. Learning about white balance

When shooting in JPEG, which is recommended as above for beginners, you need to ensure that you set your white balance before you procure a photo. The white balance impacts that color balance of your photographs. Sometimes, your images may have a bluish tone or something it has a red tinge. This is due to the white balance and of course you can use programs such as Photoshop to adjust the color balance; it is always simpler to get it right from your camera itself.

Different light sources give out different light wavelengths. The light from the candle and sunrise or sunset has a warmer, reddish tone whereas fluorescent lights give out bluish cooler wavelength. While our brain can decipher this and recognize the white surface as a white surface, the camera cannot and is not as intelligent. The camera will record blue tones and red tones and orange tones unless programmed otherwise.

There are some presets in your camera that can help overcome this differentiation of colors. The 'auto' feature (also known as auto WB or AWB) will endeavor to forecast the intensity of the light by detecting the dominant color of the scene and then contradict it. However, it may not necessarily make a correct judgment, leaving you with inaccurate colors.

Camera Guide

You need to set the color balance before taking images and just to make sure:

- Fluorescent – The green and blue tones from fluorescent lighting are neutralized with warmer tones

- Cloudy – when there is an overcast, you need to balance the warm, orange tones to enhance the daylight images.

- Daylight – utilized on sunny and radiant days. Clear days always provide neutral lighting to any photos.

- Shade – when there is shade, the lighting produced is cooler making tones of blue. Warming up the tones will help reduce the imbalance and produce a neutral color.

- Tungsten – When shooting indoors or under street lights or incandescent light bulbs. Balance out the yellow tones.

- Flash – the flash will add a relaxed blue cast to the image, so used to add some warmth.

The idea here is to avoid auto white balance and set it manually on your own. Practicing this on a regular basis will eventually become second nature to you.

Conclusion

These are all the basic and standard settings that you will get in your camera especially when you do not want to depend on the Auto function.

All these settings need to be learned over time and understanding each of its effects will have you in full control of your camera in no time. Do not attempt to learn and use

Chapter 3- Learning How to Use Your First DSLR

everything immediately. Photography is, after all, a visual journey and making mistakes will help you understand the process better.

The hardest step is to start using the aperture priority correctly - that is the biggest and most noticeable difference when taking control and directly influencing the creative process of your photos, rather than allowing your camera to decide this for you.

Once you have the aperture priority done right, you can that explore more into shutter priority and using different shooting modes and balancing both these elements.

Chapter 4:

Basics of Photography

When it comes to creative ideologies, skills, and ways of doing things, it is pretty safe to say that there are no rules. Despite that, there are a few established guidelines that take an average photograph to become a good photograph and to an amazing photographer.

These guidelines are in place so you can make the best of your camera, your skills, time and effort in taking excellent, awe-inspiring photographs and applying it in almost any kind of shooting situation.

You want to make the best out of your surroundings and taking advantage of light, shadow, object distance and so on and knowing these guidelines will help you get there.

Once you are familiar with these guidelines, you would be surprised at how easy it is to apply these techniques in various situations and how universal they are in any scenario.

1- Rule of Thirds

In this guideline, you need to imagine that your object is divided into nine equal sections by two horizontal lines and two vertical lines. The rule of thirds defines that you should position the most vital component in your scene within these lines or at least at the dots where they interconnect.

The rule of thirds ensures that you will add proper balance as well as interest to your photo resulting in a proportionate image. Some cameras that come with LCD screens already feature the rule of thirds grid, so it makes it easier for you to position your image.

2- Balancing elements

To create a more interesting photo, aligning your main subject off-center following the rule of thirds would do the trick. However, this can leave a space in the scene which can make it feel void. To counter this, you must balance the heaviness of your subject by ensuring there is another object of lesser importance to fill up the void space.

3- Leading lines

Our vision naturally focuses along lines, and this is the same when we look at photos. When taking a picture, you need to think about how you can pull viewers focus to the subject and take them through a journey. There may exist plenty of different lines such as curvy ones, diagonal lines, radial ones and zigzag ones- just not straight ones. Each of these lines can be used to improve your photo's composition.

4- Using patterns and symmetry

When taking pictures, we are surrounded by many different patterns and symmetry whether human-made or natural. They make for good compositions for your photograph, depending on how you benefit from the situation. Eye-catching compositions are an excellent way to use your photos as they can introduce tension and they can also become a focal point in your overall scene.

5- Viewpoint

If you can take the time to compose your shot, for example, taking portrait shots or engagement shots or pregnancy shots, take the time to think about where you want to shoot and which angle you want to take. Viewpoints have a tremendous impact on photo composition, and it can greatly influence the message that you want to convey in your shots. Rather than always shooting from eye level, you could consider taking shots from high ground or ground level, from the back, from the side, from close-up, and from a distance.

6- Interesting backgrounds

Any backgrounds can be made interesting depending on your angle and your viewpoint. Taking advantage of your human eye, you can easily distinguish different elements in your background scene. The camera cannot do this, and it often flattens the foreground and ruin a great photo. This problem can be easily overcome by using the right background to suit your photo needs and to convey the message that you want. Whether it is a busy background or a plain background, take the time to identify what angles to go for, so the background does not distract from your primary object or even detract from the object.

7- Depth

Photography is a two-dimensional medium, and because of that, we have to carefully choose how we want to convey the sense of depth that is present in the real-life scene. A photographer can create depth by including specific objects in the foreground, background and even middle ground. Another useful guideline to follow would be overlapping where you can intentionally obscure partially one object with another. The human eye, when looking at the photo would be able to distinguish these layers and mentally detach them, creating an image with even more depth.

8- Framing

We, as photographers can make full use of the objects that make a natural frame such as trees, holes, as well as archways. By carefully aligning these elements to frame your object, you help to separate the main subject from the surrounding world. The result you get is a more focused image that draws the natural eye's attention to the focal point of interest.

9- Cropping

Sometimes, a great photo becomes an average photo because of the lack of impact. And this is mainly because the subject in question is small and is lost among all the clutter in the background surroundings. You can crop tight around the subject to eliminate all the extra noise, thus ensuring that your subject gets the full attention of the viewer.

10- Experiment

Digital photography in the digital age has allowed us to make as many mistakes as we want because we no longer have to worry about processing the films to see how they look. We eliminate the processing cost and also eliminate the issue of running out of shots (unless you run out of memory on your card). Because of this, we can experiment as much as we want with our photos till we fully master all the composition techniques and the guidelines of photography. We can delete what we don't like and keep what we like.

Take advantage of this fact, go out there and take as many photographs as you want because you never know what composition ideas will click and you might also find a new way of taking photos.

Conclusion

Photography is a creative process as well as a science. While there are no rules, guidelines can help make the best of your effort. Sometimes these guidelines don't always work with what you have imagined in your mind for the way you want your photos to turn out, but the least you can do is consider practicing these guidelines till you have mastered them. You never know where it might lead you to and you never know what you might learn more.

Chapter 5:

Composition Guidelines

A composition is very important in photography. A poor composition can make a perfectly amazing subject appear dull, but an excellent composition can make any flat image amazing, even in the most ordinary of situations.

You must be able to understand the basics of photo-taking and photo composition.

Why is photo composition important?

- It creates astounding photos
- It helps you deliver a more compelling story
- It makes your photos look more professional
- It helps you attain balance
- It helps you take unique pictures
- It gives your photos personality
- It adds more life to your images, even if the images are black and white
- It allows your focal points to stand out

- You can capture the essence of the image more beautifully
- It awes your viewers

So, what is photo composition?

A composition refers to the placement of objects and elements in any work of art, whether visual arts, music, literature, and dance. A good composition is one that has just the right amount of detail- too few elements and the piece is bad.

Photo composition refers to composing an image by arranging specific elements in a way that complements the core of the idea or goal of your work in the best way possible.

The purpose of composing a photo is to guide the viewer's eye towards the most important aspect of your photo whether directly to the focal point or in a specific order.

Here are ten must follow guidelines to follow to help you elevate your photography game.

1- You don't need to make it complicated

While there are guidelines, it is only meant to help you understand how best to position your subject and also take advantage of lighting. That said, applying too much attention to rules and guidelines will only take away the spontaneity of the photos. When you do take photos in real scenarios, you would be working with objects and scenes that are beyond your control, and this is where the rule book needs to be removed. You must work with an open-mind and harness your creativity as well as your instinct.

Chapter 5- Composition Guidelines

What you have been practicing using the guidelines will not necessarily work for every photo you take. The important thing to take note of would be how to make the best decisions regarding composition and how these decisions will affect your final shot and how people will perceive your photos.

Choosing the focal length, framing the shot as well as the position of the subject makes all the difference.

Of course, technical know-how and guidelines are all important in photography, but you also need visual knowledge and a keen sense of instinct as well as a bit of luck- being at the right place at the right time.

2- Filling in your frame of work

Shooting large-scale scenes and scenarios can be a difficult task because you are not sure how big your subject should be in the shooting frame and how much of zoom you should apply. One of the biggest compositional mistakes would be leaving too much of space in your scene- your subject looks smaller than it is and viewers looking at your photo will be confused as to what is it that they are supposed to focus on.

To avoid this, you either get closer to the subject, or you zoom just enough to fill your shooting frame.

The first solutions of moving closer help you identify more interesting bits about your subject whereas the second solution flattens the shooting perspective and it also makes it easier for you to control or eliminate background noise.

3- Aspect ratio

When you take photos, probably the first angle you hold your camera would be horizontal. This is very common, and the truth is, it is straightforward to get stuck in this rut and cause you some creative drain.

So, to get out of this, try angling your camera to take a vertical shot instead and adjust your position and the zoom setting to experiment with a new style. Also, by cropping the image later, you can enhance the horizontal or vertical shot you've taken. When cropping, try a 16:9 ratio for a wide-screen effect or even a square shape (pretty popular these days) when using a medium-format camera.

Also, when you aren't sure which is best, take both horizontal and vertical shots. That is the great thing about digital cameras- you do not need to worry about running out for the film.

Also, a good thing to remember would be your camera's aspect ratio. The camera's ratio will not be the same as the paper you print on; this is why cropping your photo is important.

4- Avoiding the middle

Novice photographers who are starting out usually tend to shoot right in the center of the frame. Over time, you will notice that most of your images are static and pretty boring. A way to avoid this or counteract would be to use the Rule of Thirds. This essential guideline helps you split the image up into thirds either vertically or horizontally, and you can position your subject on these imaginary intersections. Although this is an overrated approach, it does help you learn how to position your photos to get the best of the surrounding elements in the frame.

You can also just move your subject away from the center and get a feel how all the elements would balance out in the frame

Chapter 5- Composition Guidelines

such as contrasting color as well as light. Again, there are no hard and fast rules to attempting to achieve this visual balance but the most quickly you rely on your instincts, the faster you will be able to identify when something looks right.

Shifting balance is often one of the ways to make your photos interesting and add another layer of perspective. Also, do not be a slave to the 'Rule of Thirds'- it is a guideline. Not following it for every shot will not result in bad photos. Also, when shooting, look out for elements to balance your scene.

5- Leading focal points

Poorly composed photographs do not have direction. This means that it does not lead the viewer's line of vision to focus on the central point- it doesn't give a clear idea of where to look hence their attention might drift somewhere else.

Using lines to control the viewer's line of sight would help you avoid this mistake.

Converging lines give the photo a strong sense of perspective as well as a three-dimensional depth. Viewers are drawn to the focal point when looking at your photo.

Curved lines, on the other hand, lead the viewer to a journey around the frame and finally to the main focal point.

Both types of lines help command a powerful guideline for viewer's line of sight. These lines exist everywhere and the photographer, it is your job to look at the details. They can be present in the form of roads, tracks, walls, buildings and even telephone lines. Finding these lines can be very important and crucial compositional elements that elevate a simple picture to an extraordinary one.

6- Using diagonals

Lines are vital to a photo. When you use horizontal lines, the image has a static yet calming feeling. Vertical lines often excuse stability as well as permanence. Diagonal lines when used in a picture, introduces the sense of drama, uncertainty as well as movement.

To get this, all it sometimes requires is a shifting of position or a focal length. Wider angles tend to bring in diagonal lines because the perspective is increased and you will be more likely to tilt your camera either downwards or upwards to get more of a scene.

Diagonal lines can also be introduced artificially using the 'Dutch Tilt' technique. All you need to do is tilt your camera as you take your shot. Although this is an effective method, it isn't a suitable element for every shot. If you want movement or force, employ the use of diagonal lines.

7- Space to move

Photographs, even though static has the power to convey a sense of movement. It is evident when we look at pictures of waves or people running or a building crumbling down that we get a sense of imbalance or a feeling of unease or a need for speed when we look at the photo. So, by creating a sense of space, you allow your subject to 'move.' For example, a speeding car needs space to show that it is moving- this would mean you would need to elongate the road the car is driving on. Runners in a marathon would also require road space to show the perspective of movement. Using diagonals here would be useful in creating both spaces as well as movement.

Chapter 5- Composition Guidelines

8- Utilizing backgrounds

What is happening in the background is also vital as it will become a great emphasis for your photo. This element ties in with simplifying of the scene as well as filling in the frame. You can't eliminate background, but you can control it.

Sometimes, just changing the position of the subject itself is enough to reduce the cluttered noise from the background. Sometimes, it is often finding an environment that complements your subject. You can also utilize wide lens aperture and a longer focal length to blur out the background behind your subject. It all depends entirely on how your background lends itself to the story you want to convey in your photo.

Getting the background right, no matter how dull it may be, can also make or break your photo. Busy and distracted backgrounds can be thrown out of focus by using long focal lengths and wider lens aperture. Reduce the space for your background so you can remove unwanted clutter. Also, positioning your camera at the right angle can also help eliminate unnecessary background.

9- Getting creative with colors

We know how colors can affect a photo. Bright colors from the primary group can attract the attention of the viewer especially when they contract with a complementing hue.

As the photographer, you have so many other ways of creating contrasting colors such as using bright splashes against monochromatic backgrounds, using vibrant patterns against a contrasting subject and also using elements of nature.

Single hues scenes can also be effective such as the harmonious shades of the setting sun, softly lit landscapes of greenery as well as the brownish hues of sand. The objective here is to be selective on how you want to isolate these colors and frame your subject.

10- Break all the rules

Photography is a visual language- you use your photos to convey a message. However, just as how we use words to create a consciously jarring effect, we can apply the same with photos by breaking with customary composition conventions.

However, you don't do it by accident. Understanding the rules of composition is one thing and then breaking them on purpose to get to a different journey is an interesting one. Breaking one rule at a time to experiment is the way to go.

Since photography is a visual language, instinct counts a lot. Understanding composition helps you use the language, but your instinct, your own creativeness, ideas, and skills allow you to connect and 'speak' to your audience through your photos.

Conclusion

Before you think that good composition equates to the most pleasing elements of the eye, think again. You might also think that the ultimate goal of applying a composition to a photo is to showcase your subject in the most aesthetically pleasing and flattering manner.

But not every work of art is supposed to be pleasing or beautiful. Different photographers want to express different ideas and motives, and they want their subjects to convey these ideas.

Chapter 5- Composition Guidelines

The photographer might want their subject to convey feelings of uneasiness or nervousness so they might come up with something shocking or unexpected such as war photography.

Using the same example, the photographer might also want to convey war victims in a disturbing and hauntingly beautiful way and may portray their subjects as being kind and compassionate against the grotesque nature of war.

In the end, the goal of composition is to express the idea the photographer has using whatever means possible- proper positioning, angle, lines, light, and focus.

Chapter 6:

Useful Photo Editing Software

Ask any photographer or designer what is the best photo editing software out there, and Photoshop will most likely be the software with the biggest votes. While Photoshop is the most powerful, needs of photographers have changed from just being able to edit images and change composition.

Photoshop isn't the most required if you need creative inspiration. Yes, it can create any effect you want but to use Photoshop is to know already what you want your resulting image to be.

What about if you need a creative inspiration? What if you need a software or program to organize your photos? Sure, you have Adobe Bridge, but Adobe Bridge is only useful as a photo browser, not so much as a cataloging tool.

What other rival applications and programs can hold a candle to Photoshop, or even do a better job? Here are ten editing tools that you can use as a beginner photographer.

1. **Adobe Photography plan**

    Platform: Mac and PC

    Image-editing: Yes

Cataloguing: Yes

Raw conversion: Yes

Adobe moved on from having to install its software to a subscription service called Adobe Creative Cloud or Adobe CC. The starting price was rather steep, but now that people have moved on to the concept of using cloud systems the price has dropped somewhat. An annual subscription to Adobe Lightroom and Photoshop is at $11 a month.

There is a special tab for photographers which feature both Lightroom and Photoshop, and you do need both programs. Photoshop is sophisticated software, but it also has its limitations. Photoshop is great for creating layers, selections, masks, retouching as well as multi-step imaging processes that no other software can compete with. The fact that is has an efficient, clean and fast interface is also another plus point.

What Photoshop doesn't do is offer an organizing system of single-click creative effects. Photoshop has all the required tools you could want in photo manipulation and editing, but it doesn't show you how to do it. That's where Lightroom comes in. Lightroom and Photoshop go hand in hand- that is why they are offered together in the package.

Lightroom combines Adobe Camera Raw's editing tools with an image cataloging database. With Lightroom, you can make non-permanent adjustments to any image which means you can always go back and change it. Your original files are never modified. Both these programs from Adobe's Creative Cloud complement each other and is recommended for any photographer planning to make photography into a business.

2. Phase One Capture One Pro 10

Platform: Mac and PC

Image-editing: Limited

Cataloguing: Yes

Raw conversion: Yes

When it first begins, Capture One was just a subsidiary software tool for Phase One's professional medium-format cameras. But since then, it has evolved into a powerful image editing and RAW conversion tool for any photographer- novice or professional.

With Capture One, you can also import your images to a searchable and centralized database and just like Lightroom; you can apply non-permanent editing and preset effects to your images. The original images are never touched or directly modified, and you can only make it permanent when you export your TIFF or JPEG versions.

This program offers more than just the common specifications and tools. Capture One's RAW conversions are excellent, and they provide a visibly sharper image with less noise compared to Adobe Camera Raw.

3. Serif Affinity Photo

Platform: Mac

Image-editing: Yes

Cataloguing: No

Raw conversion: Yes

Serif Affinity Photo is exclusively for Mac users who do not require Lightroom's capability. This software is well-known as the developer of PhotoPlus, Window's budget creative application.

Serif also offers professional Mac software together with the Affinity range. Users would find that a few of the processors as well as the terms a little different but if you can use and have mastered Photoshop; it doesn't take you too long to figure out Serif. Affinity Photo's biggest benefit is that it has been built from the ground up and also the price is a steal.

4. Adobe Photoshop Elements 15

Platform: Mac and PC

Image-editing: Yes

Cataloguing: Yes

Raw conversion: Yes

Photoshop Elements is novice friendly especially for those who have never used any editing software before. It is the amateur version of Photoshop, and while friendly, many of the advanced features found in Photoshop is left out with this release. The biggest draw for Elements used to be the tremendous price difference to Photoshop, but with Photoshop CC and Lightroom being offered at $11 per month, it does make sense to have Photoshop and its full range of features compared to Elements.

However, Elements does cater to a variety of users and novice users, and non-professionals benefit from it more than anyone else. However, its cost benefit has been taken away due to the CC deal.

5. Cyberlink PhotoDirector 8 Ultra

Platform: Mac and PC

Image-editing: Yes

Cataloguing: Yes

Raw conversion: Yes

Cyberlink PhotoDirector and Lightroom are not worlds apart. The primary image window features a selection of viewing modes, and you can also choose the most comfortable and convenient setting for yourself for image processing and photo browsing. The interface is categorized into Library, Adjustment, Edit, Layers, Slideshow, and Print. All of these features are placed below the main interface menu bar. The Adjustment feature is similar to the Develop features found in Lightroom. The tools offered in PhotoDirector are more or less what you would find in Lightroom as well, such as the radial filter effects.

One thing that takes PhotoDirector one step ahead is the Edit panel that offers a variety of effects that you would not find in Lightroom. These features make it possible for you to turn a RAW image to a finished image right within the Photo Director application itself.

6. MacPhun Luminar 1.0

Platform: Mac

Image-editing: Yes

Cataloguing: No

Raw conversion: Yes

Macphun with its weirdly sounding name is a compelling software that incorporates a single-click presets with back-end adjustments, and this is good news to both experts and photography and design enthusiast. Luminar is a fun, intelligent and rather affordable software that you can use as a standalone and simple photo-editing tool. This can also double-up as a plug-in for Photoshop, Aperture, Lightroom, and Elements and also as an editing extension for Apple Photos.

Luminar has a wealth of advanced controls and a sleek, adaptive interface which users will enjoy, especially with the one-click presets.

7. **MacPhun Creative Kit 2016**

Platform: Mac

Image-editing: Yes

Cataloguing: No

Raw conversion: (via Mac OS)

Another MacPhun offer that can also work as a standalone tool or as a plug-in for Aperture, Lightroom, and Photoshop. Some of the practical tools are Noiseless and Snapheal which is easy to use to remove noise and objects. Intensify can easily add drama and contrast to your images while Tonality is great at giving your photos the mono-retro effects. If you want to add in Bokeh quickly without going through the use of many tools, then Focus and tilt-shift in this Creative Kit can do the job. The FX photo is also another tool that provides a variety of photo effects with subtlety and depth.

8. ON1 Photo 10

Platform: PC and Mac

Image-editing: Yes

Cataloguing: Folder browsing and albums

Raw conversion: Yes

When it first began, ON1 was a success with its variety of Photoshop plug-ins, but now, it has been developed as a standalone, self-contained photo-suite of apps. This new edition, names Photo 10 integrates quick and easy edits and an excellent range of preset enhancement, effects, filters as well as corrections. It also has good portrait retouching services and different export options. The main advantage and benefit would be the array of effects that combine presets with fine-tuning capabilities.

The layer system found in Photo 10 also combines package which gives it a benefit compared to that found in Lightroom. Photo 10 is an all-rounder program with value for the price it is sold for.

9. Corel PaintShop Pro X8

Platform: PC only

Image-editing: Yes

Cataloguing: Folder browsing

Raw conversion: Yes

PaintShop was developed to rival the versatility and image editing power found in Photoshop. However, PaintShop has also been designed to make it easy to use and for it to be much more affordable compared to Photoshop. While most of

Photoshop's useful tools are found in PaintShop, they work a little different. However, for the novice user as well as professionals, it won't take them too long to adapt. The Learning Center is also there to help. The X8's version also comes with speed enhancement but some tools have deemed the software sluggish, and there's also the price which is not competitive.

Back then, PaintShop was preferred to Photoshop because it cost a fraction of what Photoshop was, but again, with the Creative Cloud, it pushes PaintShop's affordability out the window.

10. DxO Optics Pro 10

Platform: Mac and PC

Image-editing: Limited

Cataloguing: No

Raw conversion: Yes

As a designer or photographer that uses a variety of design tools, you would know that not all RAW conversion tools are created equally, and DxO is one such example. Optics Pro also began as a tool for editing and correcting chromatic aberration, distortion, edge softness as well as a vignette. Now, this program has been developed also to include a host of sophisticated RAW conversion tools that give designers a dynamic range and color information as well as maximum definition.

The program also offers a high range of color and tone adjustments, but there are no localized adjustments found.

Chapter 6- Useful Photo Editing Software

On the benefit side, the conversion produces astounding results, but on the low side, you still need other editing programs to organize your images as well as to manipulate them.

Conclusion

While Photoshop and Lightroom are the biggest and most sought-after software for editing, manipulating as well as organizing, many other programs, and software and chasing the coveted title as well and are continuously improving and developing their programs to meet designers and photographers demands.

It is always a good idea to try other software and programs out there because you never know what tool and feature they might introduce that would make your editing easier.

Conclusion

Thank you for making it through to the end of *Camera Guide: Learn What Your Digital Camera Has to Offer*. Hopefully, this book has shed light on the basics that you need to get started on using your digital camera to its fullest. Remember to also read your manual to see if there are any features not found in this book since all cameras are not created equal.

Investing in a digital camera whether a point-and-shoot, DSLR or Mirrorless also requires investment in how to use it too.

Knowledge on how to use the camera properly in order to get the most out of it is essential. Even the most basic cameras require that you understand your product. You should also purchase a camera based on your needs and requirement. For example, if superior shots and printing large photos is what you want, then a DSLR or Mirrorless would do the trick.

If just recording memories of your trips, travels or documenting things is what you need a camera for, then a point-and-shoot is sufficient.

If taking selfies and wefies, food photos and just about anything that comes your way in order to upload them on social media, then a camera-phone does the job.

Camera Guide

Understanding the basic functions of your camera will ensure that you get the best photo in any lighting conditions and you would also be able to fine tune how to use aperture, shutter speed and ISO like a professional. The same is true for even a camera phone.

How you angle the camera, how you position your camera, and how the subject is framed within an image all help in creating a fantastic photo.

Finally, if you found this book useful in any way, a review on Amazon is always appreciated!

www.ingramcontent.com/pod-product-compliance
Lightning Source LLC
Chambersburg PA
CBHW050018230526
45470CB00003B/1028